IN THE FULLNESS OF TIME

A Christmas Celebration of Emmanuel's Coming

BY RICHARD KINGSMORE

WITH DRAMATIC SCENES BY NAN GURLEY

LILLENAS
PUBLISHING COMPANY

lillenas.com

CONTENTS

CAST

GRAMMY	High-spirited grandmother in her 60's
LENA	GRAMMY's 12-year-old grandchild
MOM	offstage voice only

(As CHRISTMAS IS THE BEST TIME OF THE YEAR *begins, the lights come up on a simple living room setting with a partially decorated Christmas tree.* GRAMMY *enters carrying a huge box. It contains gifts, wrapping paper, scissors, scotch tape, ribbon, empty boxes for wrapping the gifts, Christmas decorations, and an unopened nativity scene. The gifts are: an old pocket watch, an African drum, a pearl necklace, an old Bible, a huge dog bone, and a small box for earrings.* GRAMMY *takes everything out of the box and places them on a large table. She begins getting organized to wrap her gifts. Throughout the musical,* GRAMMY *and* LENA *will wrap the gifts. By the end of the musical, each gift will be wrapped and placed under the tree. By the end of* CHRISTMAS IS THE BEST TIME OF THE YEAR, *Grammy has everything on the table and Lena enters.)*

Christmas Is the Best Time of the Year

with
Deck the Halls
Jingle Bells

Words and Music by
PAUL JOHNSON
Arranged by Richard Kingsmore

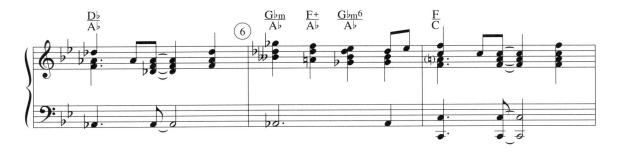

10

14

Christ - mas.

*"Jingle Bells"

86 Solo
mf

Dash - ing thro' the snow   in a one - horse o - pen sleigh,

O'er the fields we go,   laugh - ing all the way.

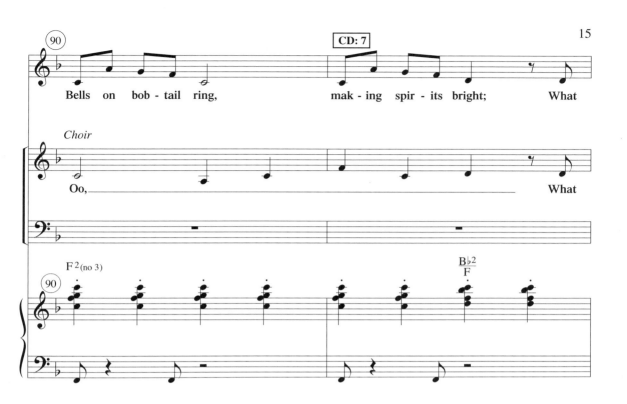

Bells on bob-tail ring, mak-ing spir-its bright; What

Choir

Oo,_____ What

fun it is to laugh and sing a sleigh-ing song to-night!

fun it is to laugh and sing a sleigh-ing song to-night!

O

Christ - mas. Cho - irs sing of our Re - deem - er's birth. Wrap up your pres - ents, re - live your ad - o -

Scene 1

LENA: Grammy! I'm so glad you're here!

GRAMMY: Lena! Give me a hug! *(they hug)* Merry Christmas!

LENA: Merry Christmas to you too! How long can you stay?

GRAMMY: I'm here till New Year's Day.

LENA: Good! That gives us plenty of time to go to the mall!

GRAMMY: That sounds wonderful!

LENA: What are you doing?

GRAMMY: Wrapping my gifts. I'm especially excited about it because this Christmas I'll be giving each of you a part of your inheritance.

LENA *(holds the pocket watch)*: Who's this for?

GRAMMY: O now this is a special one. It's for your Daddy. This pocket watch belonged to my grandfather.

LENA: O yeah, I've seen some old pictures of him. He always wore that funny hat.

GRAMMY *(takes the watch from Lena and gently holds it)*: I can remember when I was a little girl we'd go to visit him and I'd always say, "Granddaddy, what time is it?" just so I could see the watch, and very slowly he'd pull this watch out of his pocket and say, "Well now, little girl, what's your hurry?"

LENA: It's beautiful. *(Music begins)*

GRAMMY: Your Daddy always admired it. And I think this Christmas is just the right time to give it to him. *(They wrap the watch together throughout* WHEN CHRISTMAS COMES THIS YEAR *and place it under the tree.)*

When Christmas Comes This Year

Words and Music by
ROBERT WHITE JOHNSON
and JIM ROBINSON
Arranged by Richard Kingsmore

lis - ten close____ you'll hear, Voic - es sing - ing hope____

____ for ev - 'ry - one.____ A-round the

fire____ burn - ing bright With our loved ones here to-night,____ We'll

CD: 13

32

Scene 2

GRAMMY: Here, help me with this. *(Together, they open the box of ornaments and place them on the Christmas tree throughout the following dialogue.)*

LENA: Grammy, I wish I was older.

GRAMMY: O now, don't rush it. You'll get there soon enough.

LENA: My parents won't let me do anything. Every time I ask them if I can do something, they always say, "Not yet!"

GRAMMY: Now aren't you exaggerating a little?

LENA: No I'm not! I'll prove it. Listen. *(calling)* Hey Mom, can I get my ears pierced?

MOM *(offstage)*: Not yet.

LENA: See what I mean?

GRAMMY: Well, at least she didn't say no. Not yet is a good answer! At least it's full of hope that the answer you want is definitely coming at some point!

LENA: But they just don't trust me! Watch this. Hey Mom, can I go to the movies with my friends?

MOM *(offstage)*: Not yet.

LENA: See? She just doesn't understand.

GRAMMY: Yes, she does. Your mother had to wait for things when she was your age and she didn't always get the things she wanted when she wanted them.

LENA: What did she have to wait for?

GRAMMY: Well I remember when your mother was in high school, some of her friends planned a ski trip to Colorado on their Christmas break. Your mother wanted to go, of course, but her father and I didn't think the time was right. We told your mother that she needed more time to prove to us that she was mature enough to do something like that.

LENA: I'm just afraid all the fun is gonna happen without me!

GRAMMY: Don't be afraid, honey. Life is all about waiting. God has a treasure house of gifts He wants to give you, *(Music begins)* but He has to wait until you're ready to fully enjoy them. The Bible says, "No good gift does He withhold from those who walk in righteousness." But the time has to be right. You wouldn't give a set of car keys to a newborn baby, now would you?

LENA: Of course not.

GRAMMY: The same is true of our Father God. He understands waiting. He waited thousands of years before the time was right to send Jesus to the earth. And He plans for every good thing to come to you at just the right time in your life. *(During* IN THE FULLNESS OF TIME, *they finish placing all the decorations on the tree.)*

Waiting
(Underscore)

RICHARD KINGSMORE

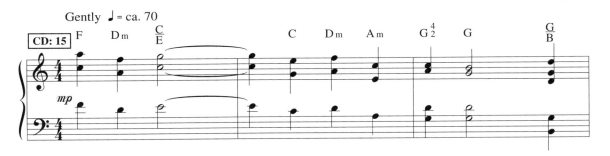

Segue to "In the Fullness of Time"

In the Fullness of Time

Words and Music by
KIRK KIRKLAND
Arranged by Richard Kingsmore

reached out His hand,_____ In the full - ness of time_____ He

F²   G²   A m²

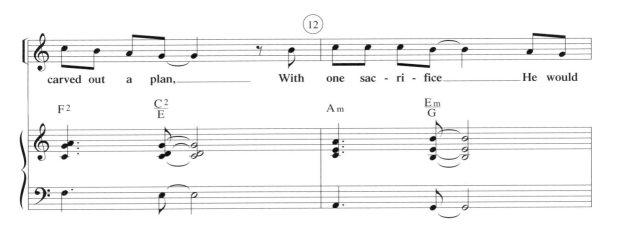

(12)

carved out a plan,_____ With one sac - ri - fice_____ He would

F²   C²/E   A m   E m/G

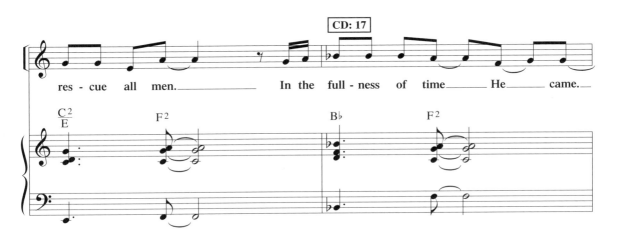

CD: 17

res - cue all men._____ In the full - ness of time_____ He_____ came._____

C²/E   F²   B♭   F²

40

CD: 18

our righ-teous-ness. In the full-ness of time He came.

And the whole world cried, "Ho -

san - na, God save us!" And heav - en re - plied, and

46

CD: 22

a - gain. And the whole world cried, "Ho - san - na, God save us!" And heav - en re - plied, and called His name Je - sus,

King of kings and Lord of lords, Em-

man - u - el, our Sav - ior is born; When the

mo - ment ar - rived to give hope a name In the

Scene 3

(At the end of IN THE FULLNESS OF TIME, Grammy *puts a beautiful African drum up on the table to be wrapped. They sit at the table together.)*

LENA: Whoa! That's cool!

GRAMMY: It's a drum from South Africa. It was given to me 37 years ago when your Grandfather and I lived there as missionaries.

LENA: Who gave it to you?

GRAMMY: A young man about your age. Even though it was so long ago, I can still hear his music. It was our first Christmas in a little village outside Johannesburg. We didn't know many people and I was lonely and homesick. On Christmas Eve, he came to our door with this drum in his arms and said, "Jambo!"

LENA: What does that mean?

GRAMMY: It means hello! He sat down and began to play this drum and sing. His sweet smile made me feel welcome. *(Music begins)* When he finished playing, I sat down beside him and began to sing Christmas carols. He played his drum and the rhythms of Africa blended with "Silent Night" and "Joy to the World." Then I drew some pictures for him of Jesus in the manger, then Jesus on the cross, and the empty tomb, and I told him the story of salvation. He was my first friend in Africa and from that moment I began to feel at home.

LENA: Who are you giving it to?

GRAMMY: Well, I thought it would be the perfect gift for your big brother. Michael told me he's always dreamed of going to Africa.

LENA: Yeah, he talks about it all the time.

GRAMMY: I thought this drum might stir up the fire in his heart and inspire him. When he holds a little piece of South Africa in his arms, maybe he'll be able to imagine himself there, sharing Jesus with everyone he meets. (LENA *and* GRAMMY *wrap the drum in Christmas paper during* O COME, O COME, EMMANUEL *and place it under the tree.)*

Silent Night! Holy Night!

(Underscore)

FRANZ GRUBER
Arranged by Richard Kingsmore

Segue to "O Come, O Come, Emmanuel"

O Come, O Come, Emmanuel

Latin Hymn

Plainsong
Arranged by Richard Kingsmore

come, come a-dore___ Him. Come a-dore___ Him,

come, come a-dore___ Him. Come a-dore___ Him,

CD: 26

come, come a-dore___ Him.

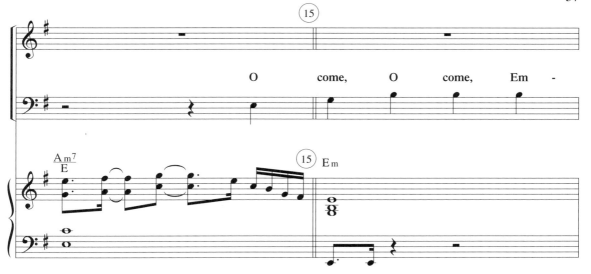

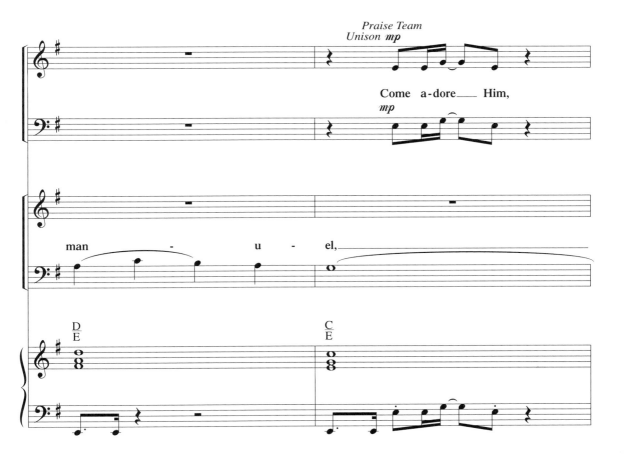

58

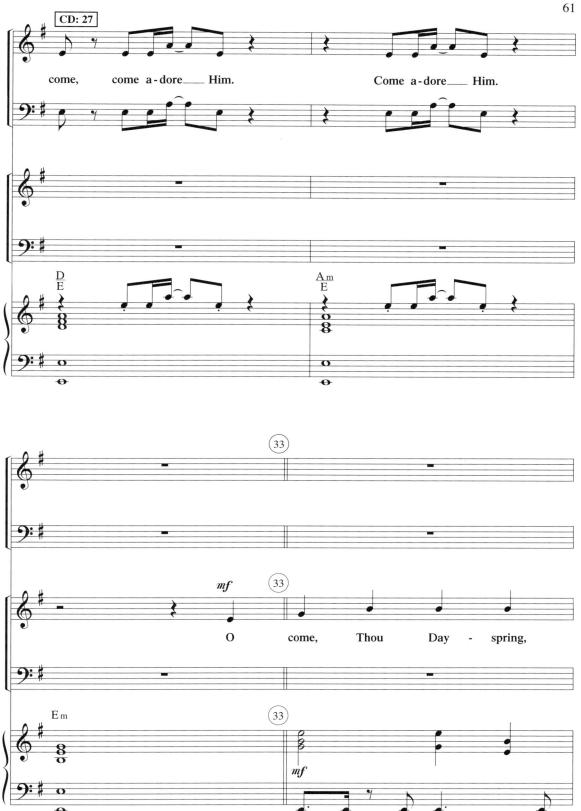

64

Scene 4

GRAMMY *(holding a pearl necklace)*: Now here's something your Mother has had to wait for a long time.

LENA: What is it?

GRAMMY: The pearl necklace I wore on my wedding day. I felt like a princess. I was dressed in a white linen gown and wore a veil that reached to the floor. My mother placed these pearls around my neck and said, "I'm proud of you, honey. Today is a day you've dreamed of for a long time. You waited for God to bring this man into your life. He is God's gift to you and you are God's perfect gift to him, given at just the right time."

LENA: Let's use white paper and gold ribbon.

GRAMMY: All right. I'll bet one day your Mother will give this necklace to you. When the time is right.

LENA: Grammy, why are you giving away all your cool stuff?

GRAMMY: Well, the older I get, the more thankful I am to God for letting me share *(music begins)* in the inheritance of Jesus and in the riches of His glory. I know beyond any doubt how much God loves me because of what He's given me. So I guess I'm trying to do the same thing. I'm giving my treasures to my loved ones to show them how much I love them. *(Together they wrap the necklace during* HOLY LOVE *and place it under the tree.)*

Holy Love

with
The First Noel

Words and Music by
ROBERT WHITE JOHNSON
and JIM ROBINSON
Arranged by Richard Kingsmore

PLEASE NOTE: Copying of this product is NOT covered by CCLI licenses. For CCLI information call 1-800-234-2446.

84

*"The First Noel"

CD: 37

92

CD: 38

Scene 5

GRAMMY: Here, help me with this. *(Opens a box containing the pieces of a nativity scene.)*

LENA: A nativity scene! *(They begin unwrapping each piece and setting up the nativity scene.)*

GRAMMY: I always had this on the dining room table at Christmas time when your mother was a little girl. The whole family would gather around the table and your mother and all your uncles would set up each piece while I read the Christmas story.

LENA: Mom told me all about this.

GRAMMY: I would read, "And this will be a sign for you: you will find a baby wrapped in swaddling clothes and lying in a manger…" and then your Mom would place the baby Jesus in the manger.

LENA: And here are the shepherds.

GRAMMY: "Do not be afraid for I bring you good news! Today there has been born for you a Savior who is Christ the Lord!"

LENA: And the wise men.

GRAMMY: "And wise men came from the East bringing gold, frankincense and myrrh." We read the whole story and by the end every piece was in place.

LENA: A stable is a strange place for a king to be born.

GRAMMY: Yes. When I look at this, I think how God is good at taking small things and doing big things through them.

LENA: What do you mean?

GRAMMY: Well, before Jesus was born, nobody thought much of a place called Bethlehem.

LENA: You mean it wasn't famous?

GRAMMY *(music begins)*: Not at all. But God had promised that even though it was small among all the nations, something very important was going to happen there. It was going to be the birthplace of the Messiah. And at just the right time in history, Jesus was born in Bethlehem.

LENA: So I guess small can also be important?

GRAMMY: Absolutely.

LENA: That's good news when you're only twelve. *(They laugh together)* *(During* DOWN IN BETHLEHEM, *they finish setting up the nativity scene.)*

Down in Bethlehem

Words and Music by
JOHN DARIN ROWSEY
Arranged by Richard Kingsmore

101

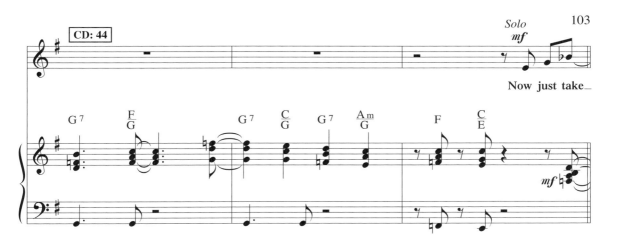

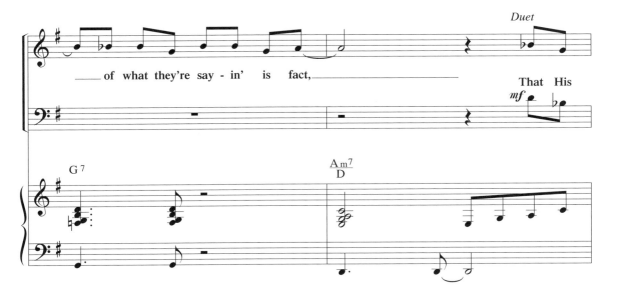

110

-by came to save the world. _____ They

say He is the Son of God, the Great I_____ Am, And it's

got the whole town in a whirl._____ I heard____

114

Scene 6

(GRAMMY and LENA sit at the table.)

GRAMMY: You know, Lena, you've got a lot of exciting things ahead of you.

LENA: I want to get my ears pierced on my 13th birthday, but I don't think Mom's gonna let me. She's always in such a good mood when you're here. I was thinking maybe you could talk to her and get her to let me do it.

GRAMMY: We'll see. Here. Help me wrap this. *(reaches for an old worn Bible)*

LENA: What is it?

GRAMMY: It was your grandfather's Bible. I'm giving it to your big sister.

LENA *(rubbing her hand across the cover)*: It's so old.

GRAMMY: Your grandfather read aloud from it every night before we went to sleep. It's full of little notes in the margins and places he underlined.

LENA *(opens the Bible)*: Look. He marked this verse with a red pen. "I can do all things through Christ who strengthens me." Why did he mark that one?

GRAMMY: That verse became your grandfather's favorite while we were in South Africa. It taught him that the word of God really does have the power to change you!

LENA: What happened?

GRAMMY: There was another village close to the one where we lived. The people there were not friendly with the people of our village. We were told never to go near them or talk to them. One day, we learned that the daughter of the chief in the other village was very sick and might be dying. We had medicine that we thought might help her, so your grandfather told the people of our village that he was going there to try and help. They begged him not to go and warned him of the danger, but he went anyway.

LENA: Did the chief's daughter live?

GRAMMY: Yes. The medicine worked. And soon the people of both villages began to be friends.

LENA: That was very brave.

GRAMMY: Your grandfather told me he kept repeating that verse over and over as he walked to the village and it gave him courage.

LENA: Why are you giving this Bible to Mary? *(Music begins)*

GRAMMY: Your grandfather had a passion for the Scriptures. He loved to tell people about Jesus. Mary has that same passion and I know she will cherish this Bible as much as her grandfather did. *(They wrap the Bible during* CHANGE THE WORLD *and place it under the tree.)*

Change the World

Words and Music by
KENN MANN and
TURNER LAWTON
Arranged by Richard Kingsmore

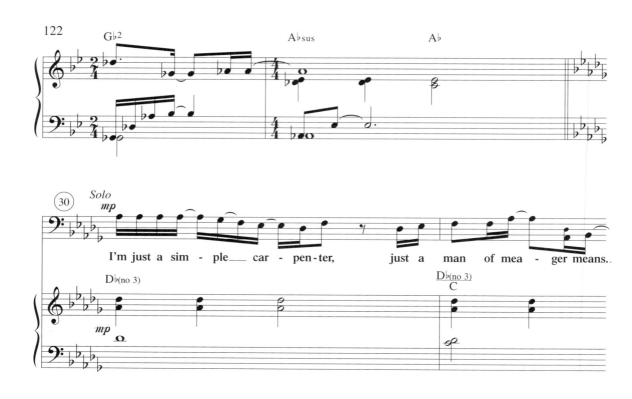

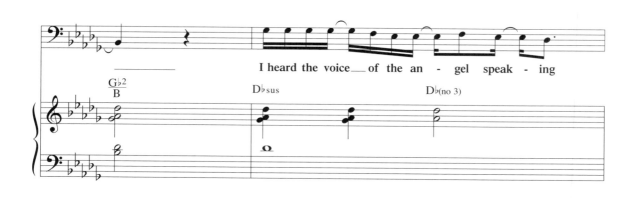

Who would have ev - er thought,_____ Who would have ev-

plan,_____ Oo,_____

Ab   Db2/F   Ab/Gb   Gb2   Db2/F

- er dreamed,_____ That I would be_____ the one_____ to be a

ev - er dreamed,_____

Ebm11   Ab7/C   Db2   Ab/Gb   Gb2   Db2/F

128

Scene 7

GRAMMY: And now I think there's one more person whose gift we haven't wrapped yet.

LENA: Mine?

GRAMMY: That's right. *(Reaches for a small box)* Are you gonna help me wrap it?

LENA: Of course! What is it?

GRAMMY: Oh, I'm not telling. You have to wait just like everybody else.

LENA: I can't wait till I'm older. Then I won't have to wait for anything! *(Music begins)*

GRAMMY: That's not true. We're all waiting for something.

LENA: What are you waiting for?

GRAMMY: Well, for one thing, I'm waiting for Jesus to smooth out some of my rough edges. I'm still what you might call "a work in progress." That's why I love Christmas. It fills me with hope and reminds me that God is never finished. He'll never give up on me. He always loves me and He's making me more like Jesus every day. If the miracle of Bethlehem lives in me, then all things are possible! *(During* CHRISTMAS OF HOPE, *they wrap* LENA's *gift and place it under the tree.)*

Hope
(Underscore)

RICHARD KINGSMORE

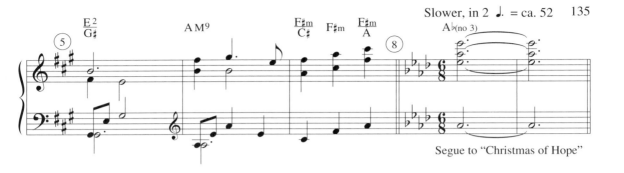

Segue to "Christmas of Hope"

Christmas of Hope

Words and Music by
BUDDY MULLINS
and REBECCA J. PECK
Arranged by Richard Kingsmore

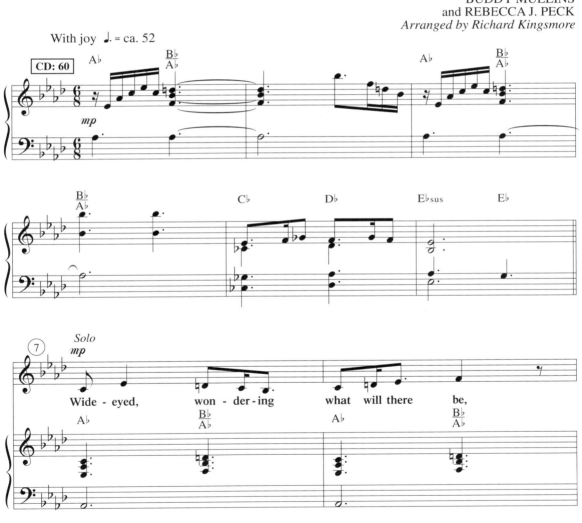

Wide - eyed,   won - der-ing   what   will there   be,

PLEASE NOTE: Copying of this product is NOT covered by CCLI licenses. For CCLI information call 1-800-234-2446.

Just what's wait - ing there un - der the tree?

How do we cap - ture the mag - ic we find

There in the face___ of a child?___

Once more turn - ing our hearts to be - lieve,

Looking past what we've chosen to see,

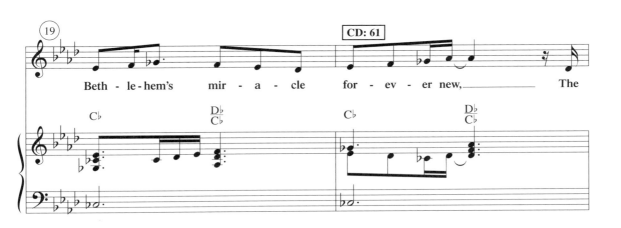

Bethlehem's miracle forever new,_____ The

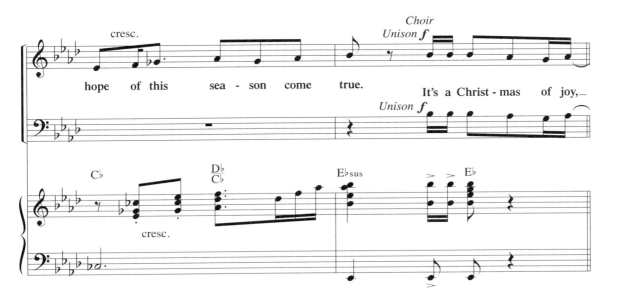

hope of this season come true. It's a Christmas of joy,___

2nd time to Coda
(to pg. 142, meas. 52)
Unison

This is a Christ - mas of hope.

CD: 62

All of the trim - mings of hol - i - day cheer

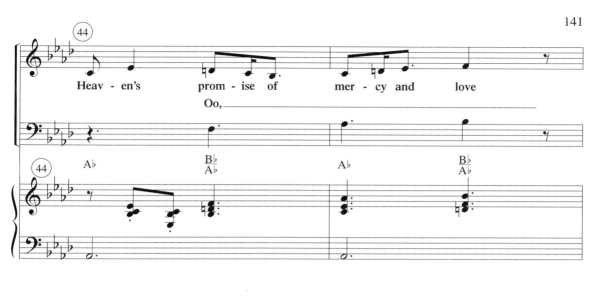

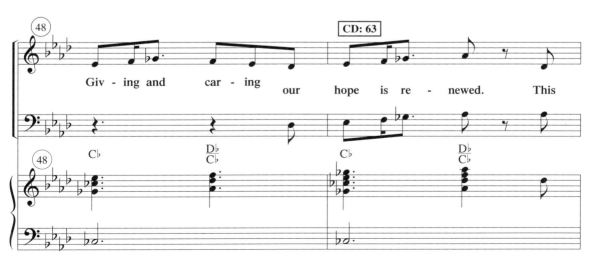

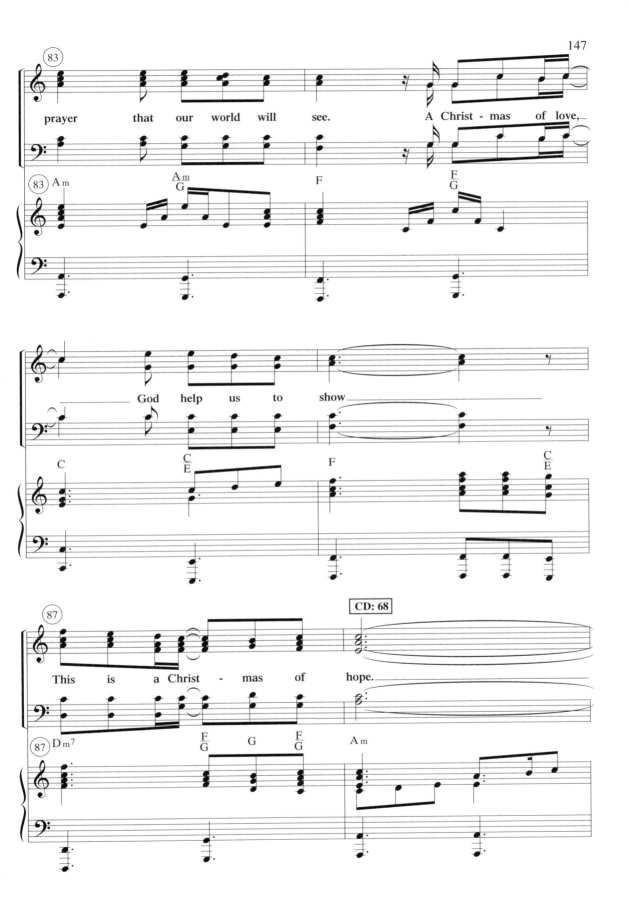

Scene 8

GRAMMY: Guess who this is for? *(Reveals a huge dog bone)*

LENA: Brownie!

GRAMMY: No one gets left out on Christmas day. You choose the paper.

LENA: What's that wonderful smell?

GRAMMY: I think it's your Mom's good cooking.

LENA: Great! I'm hungry. *(calling offstage)* Hey Mom! Is dinner ready?

MOM *(offstage)*: Not yet! *(GRAMMY and LENA look at each other and laugh)*

LENA: See what I mean? I'm stuck in the never ending "not yet"!

GRAMMY: You're not alone. You know the folks in the Bible knew what it was like to have to wait for something.

LENA: What do you mean?

GRAMMY: Well, Noah had to wait a long time for it to stop raining. Abraham and Sarah had to wait a long time before Isaac was born. And Moses had to wait a long time before he got the children of Israel to the promised land.

LENA: God must think it's important for us to learn to wait. *(Music begins)*

GRAMMY: If we never had to wait for anything, we'd never grow up.

LENA: God's people had to wait for the birth of Jesus, too.

GRAMMY: That's right. The Old Testament prophets told the people not to give up hope and to keep looking toward the day when the Messiah would be born. God's people waited for centuries. "And when the fullness of time came, God sent forth His Son, born of a woman…"

LENA: We're waiting for Jesus too, aren't we.

GRAMMY: Yes. And I have no doubt that at just the right time, He'll come again. And then all of our waiting will be over. *(During* BE NOT AFRAID, *they finish wrapping the dog bone and place it under the tree.)*

God's Plan

(Underscore)

RICHARD KINGSMORE

Segue to "Be Not Afraid"

Be Not Afraid

Words and Music by
JOHN WALLER
Arranged by Richard Kingsmore

PLEASE NOTE: Copying of this product is NOT covered by CCLI licenses. For CCLI information call 1-800-234-2446.

Sin and shame kept him a-way from re-li-gious kinds of crowds,____ He
Oo,_____ Oo,

nev-er tho't the God he sought__ would fi-nal-ly__ be found._____ Then
Oo,

Scene 9

GRAMMY: Well, young lady, I just have one question. Are you too old to sit in my lap?

LENA: Not yet. *(sits in* GRAMMY'S *lap)*

LENA: Give me just a little hint about my present.

GRAMMY: Well, let's just say, if I have any luck with your mother, you'll be wearing them on your 13th birthday!

LENA *(hugging her)*: Grammy! Thank you!

GRAMMY: You just have to wait a little bit longer.

LENA: I guess I don't feel so bad about waiting anymore. It helps to think that Jesus is waiting too.

GRAMMY: Yes. Till we're all ready to be with Him.

LENA: And till everyone knows He's the Savior.

GRAMMY: One day every knee *(music begins)* will bow and every tongue confess that He is Lord.

LENA: Now that will be a celebration!

GRAMMY: The best ever!

Hallelujah He Is Born

Words and Music by
MARK A. MILLER
and GREGG HUBBARD
Arranged by Richard Kingsmore

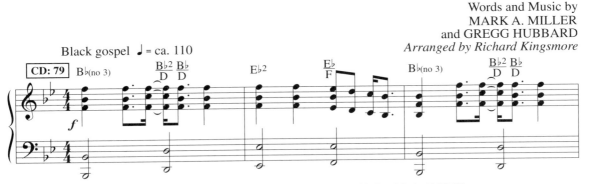

PLEASE NOTE: Copying of this product is NOT covered by CCLI licenses. For CCLI information call 1-800-234-2446.

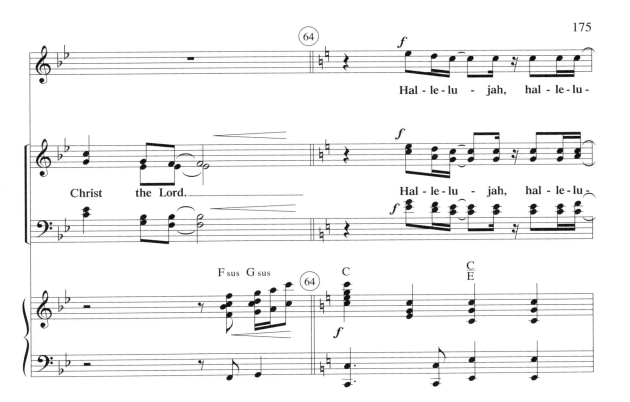

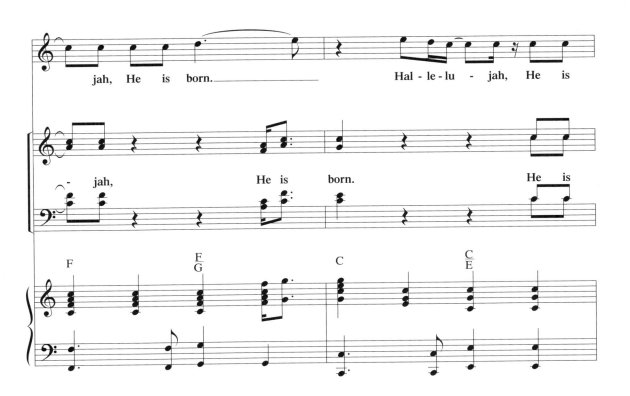

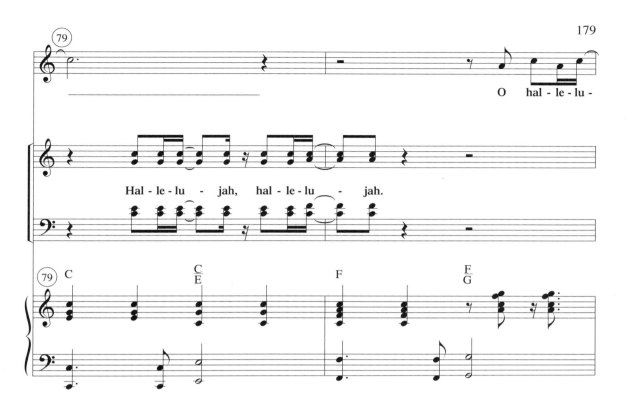

PRODUCTION NOTES

This is an easy-to-stage Christmas musical with several short scenes between GRAMMY, a wonderful Christian woman with a rich heritage, and LENA, her hopeful and longing 12-year-old granddaughter. Each scene provides segues to the music as it relates the theme of God's perfect timing throughout history and our lives.

The simple setting and small cast makes this musical accessible for churches of any size. Only two characters are required with an additional offstage female voice with a few lines throughout. The setting is a living room with a partially decorated Christmas tree and a table for wrapping gifts.

GRAMMY should be appropriate age, with a warm voice and big spirit. GRAMMY is not a frail lady, but one who still has a lot of energy and spunk. She drives the message and should be played by someone who really draws the audience in.

LENA can be cast with a slightly older girl playing a couple of years younger if necessary. Despite being a pre-teen and all that goes with it, LENA'S innocence and youthfulness really shine when she's with her grandmother. In this setting, there is little attitude, and she allows herself to be transparent and somewhat childlike.

The characters need to be comfortable with one another to communicate the warm relationship between them. Be sure to have them actually wrap each present a few times during rehearsals to get the timing down. Find creative stage business for Grammy and Lena during the songs, and if possible, take the lights down on that part of the stage area when the choir is singing.

The script is more episodic in nature, so look for ways to vary the tempo and energy levels in each scene. Give the audience variety to keep them interested in the story.